CW01065146

# the w

## Molly Nash

BookLeaf
Publishing

India | USA | UK

the waves © 2023 Molly  Nash

All rights reserved.

No part of this publication may be
reproduced, stored in a retrieval system, or
transmitted, in any form or by any means,
electronic, mechanical, photocopying,
recording or otherwise, without the prior
written permission of the presenters.

Molly  Nash asserts the moral right to be
identified as author of this work.

Presentation by *BookLeaf Publishing*

Web: www.bookleafpub.com

E-mail: info@bookleafpub.com

ISBN: 9789358318883

First edition 2023

*for Grandad,*

*from whom I continue to learn.*

# Walk with me again

Sometimes I taste the summer.
Her kiss lingers on my lips,
tasting of sea salt carried by westerly winds,
until it dissolves like
the candy floss I tasted a long time ago,
walking along the pier.

Crystallised sugar snaked
along my fingers, chin, cheeks,
Nestling even in my hairline.
As the sun dipped into the water,
I wondered if she was scared of the dark waves.
They used to scare me, too,
until my Grandad clasped my tiny, sticky hand,
in his- calloused and lined with memories.
Together, the water didn't seem so scary,
not when I had a hand to hold,
and we leapt into the sea foam and shells,
hurdled the rolling adversary,
swam with the black-tipped sharks I was sure
lurked below.
We shared fish and chips, afterwards,
and walked along the pier.

As the sun dips into the water,

and I walk along the pier
A habit trickling into the thousandth time,
the salt-kiss lingers on my lips,
and I pass a storefront older than my time.
I have conquered every fear since that day,
knowing that a calloused hand lined with love
would clasp my own, now growing lines of its
own,
and send a message beyond words
from a place none of us have yet ventured.

When I pluck a pink wisp from the stick,
I don't fight the urge to leave my shoes
collecting sand,
and I leap once more into dark, dark waves,
my hand empty,
my heart full.
Summer on my tongue.

# Dollhouse

Dollhouse
When the world waits in slumber,
How can the sky pass the time,
but by shedding the weight of the
clouds, of the birds, of the poets so bold,
and paint weaving patterns made from sunlight?
For a moment,
just before the first eyelids a-flutter,
the first slippers adorned,
the first kettles go a-whistling,
the sky can play in her dollhouse
and break away from her responsibility.
She is still young, after all,
and, for a moment,
she is free.

# hope is a buoy in a dark, dark sea

I try to search for something
that connects me to what comes after.
Some message tied with a silk ribbon
in Death's remorseful hand-
A bouy bobbing in that dark, dark sea,
A marker that says:
I lived. I was here. And I have not gone far.

Something that proves he did not hasten,
That in those last moments, Death was kind,
and he left me a reminder
that, though your body is gone,
your song still fights against the tempest,
A melody battling through the roar.

But most times it is my aching heart
straining for your voice in the echo of my cries.
It is then that I remember
how even the brightest star, as we gaze into the
night,
is already dead and cold.

Does that make it less beautiful?
Less worthwhile, less real?

Is it even there at all?
Death cannot say,
Nor, I suppose, can I:
I only know hope, and I cling to it,
desperate to stay above the water.

Like a buoy in a dark, dark sea.

# ten words

Life is birdsong and coffee and loving without
good reason

# orange juice

If you wake up in the morning
to find that I'm not there,
please do not come scrambling
or rushing down the stairs.
Instead, peel back the curtain
and peer out at fresh day:
take a breath and close your eyes
and know that I'm okay.
I know you cannot see me,
and I long to see you smile-
like always, I am with you,
and will be for a while.
If at night you can't sleep easy,
please, don't cry for me.
Think of the time we've spent together,
because that is where I'll be-
held woven in your memories,
in the golden shawl of love.
I'll wrap it around your shoulders
and hold you from above.
I know how much you loved me
and how much I love you,
now take that love and share it
as I taught you how to do.
Breathe the air of far-flung lands

and swim in every sea!
Perhaps each time you see the stars
you can pick one out for me.
So, when you wake up in the morning
to find that I'm not there,
just hold close all of our memories
and the time we got to share.

# i will keep going

i am running into the new year
i don't know what will happen
but as the years fly by
whipping my hair and catching my cheek,
i will stretch out a hand
and brush against the arm of
each person i have been
it is the end and it is not
it is the beginning and yet the starting
gun refuses to fire
but i will keep running nonetheless, and i will
run hard
come on, run with me
so that, when we fall,
there will be a hand to lift us
from the ground and set us right
take my hand and
we'll do it together
it is only life

# linger at the doorway

It is sneakily buying a book
that a friend was gushing about,
as they weighed its cost against their wages,
before deciding against it, leaving
the shop forlornly gazing at the cover.
And then it is the moment when you
slip it into their hand,
one corner ragged and dogeared
because you were so excited to buy it
that you thrust it at the cashier,
giddy with spreading love,
spending ochre, gaining ambrosia.
It is the way their face shifts
as they realise what you've done:
confusion; disbelief; joy; gratitude,
a cascading system of love
and friendship so unspoken that it
comes only in thoughts,
like a hazy dream you can't quite picture
but remember how it made you feel.

And then it is the coffee,
a soy latte with hazelnut syrup,
that they pay for with mongoose reflexes

before your fingers graze the cash in your
pocket-
the garlic bread you sneak into their oven
to compliment their tomato pasta bake.
The bottle of red wine waiting on your
countertop
and the pink-frosted cupcake on theirs.

And on it goes, never-ending,
an uncompromising vow
to love each other
so much
that you scheme, plot, contrive,
to gift the next amulet,
battling to leave the next token of love.

And so is life.
Each black and blind turn is nothing more
than an empty corner of air dressed up as a
halloween monster
and love is just a word
until someone comes into your life
and breathes into it a meaning
that words cannot express.

Life is brushing a hand in the darkness, and
holding on.
Even just for a little while.

# a haiku (1)

the music shuffles
I try to catch the song, but
it all ends so soon

# her many faces

her many faces
Grief is the shadow that love leaves behind
to remind you how one light can brighten a life.
Grief is the weight of them curled in your heart.
She waits for you on street corners, hoping you'll
one day acknowledge her.
It's okay if you don't. If you walk by,
head down, headphones on,
furiously stomping down the road until
you feel safe enough to look back.
It's okay.
Because one day, she'll let herself in the back
door
and she'll switch on the kettle,
She'll reach into the cupboard
Without asking where the sugar is kept,
Wordlessly pluck a teaspoon from the drawer.
She already knows which mug is yours,
because it's her mug too.
And she'll pull up a chair without being asked,
And she won't leave, no matter what you say,
Because she knows that, now she's here,
You don't want her to leave.
Offer her some biscuits. I think she'd like that.
Offer her a custard cream.

# who am i to answer?

It is screeching into a microphone,
words long discarded, the shrieks blasphemous
to the artist-
no rhythm nor tone,
barely even passable as sound.

And then it ebbs into the fumbling to
encase a moment forever,
to capture joy in pixels and grain,
without the polish of fixed hair and plastered
grins.
Instead, the ghosts of laughter are etched into
faces,
 droplets of cider forever immortalised before
they fell,
coating the dress in front.
I like to think it's somewhere in that melee, too.

Maybe it's piling into that smallest alcove,
where the karaoke machine buzzed away,
all craning and straining to see the lyrics.
Our bodies pressed together,
Fighting for breath and yet
not uncomfortable,
not questioning,

just souls merging into one, as they were
intended.

It is swaying to that wordless music,
The hymn of finding love and holding on
tighter than you have held anything else.
It is droning tones and desperate hugs,
hoarse throats and piled goodbyes.

It sparks and flames within us all-
glimmers and glares and gleams.
The darkness of night is lit by the stars within,
and gazing upon them is to see God's creations
for ourselves.
Beyond words, beyond definition, beyond each
of us.

We simply Are.
It simply Is.
What will be, quite simply, will Be.

# Misdirection

Outside, you hide beneath a mask so clear
but it crinkles and twists and disappears-
 the coaxing of warm hands and love is enough;
your aspects so harsh, so unbreakably rough.
And spilling from cracks is an anger that bites
one powdery, like dust from fairies or sprites.
Like snow upon sun you melt away, lost in
dream.
Your true form at last, so seldomly seen.
You are no woman, nor man, nor beast felled
from heaven...
...no one guessed...

Sherbert Lemon

# I Don't Like Poetry

I don't like poetry
It is just
Pompous words and
Melancholy ramblings,
Incoherent scrawlings
By idiots who think
Far too deeply
And share those thoughts far
Too often in
Sycophantic similies
Or alliteration peppered
Like pus-filled boils across pale skin.
It is bleak and critical,
Humourous or ironic-
No. I resent it.
Let enjambent slink away,
Its bombast tail between mangy legs.
Keep Coleridge and Keats,
Hardy and Rosetti.
Hold your caesura. Reign the iambic.
Burn your poetry.
At the very least,
Keep it away from me.

# It Is Not Written

I wait beside the cycle path
that bridges grass to sea
and when I cannot turn away,
an old thought waits for me.

Beneath the clashing clouds of grey,
the freckled rain and wind,
I watch the waves roll in to shore,
to crash and then rescind
back into grey and foaming depths
and flee from their own thunder.

I stand and, from another's eyes,
I watch myself sink under.

The grass beneath my feet is wet,
my coat and cheeks are, too,
but some place between the sand and sea
a lost heart flickers blue.

I cannot turn to face the thought,
though salt-wind bites my cheeks;
the gulls above soar and dive
and fill the air with shrieks.

I've lost so many who cross the path
to leave footprints along the beach.
By night the tides have taken them
beyond my stretching reach.

The cycle path is empty now,
and beyond it is the sand...
but, though I take a step towards,
I'm not ready to leave this land.

Thinking this I feel the thought
behind me shift and crumble.
The grey rolls back to brighter skies
and the storm fades to a rumble.

# The Gulls

Two seagulls sit on a rooftop
The slates glow red in the dying sun
but they don't take flight.
Instead, they wait and sing to
the ebbing light,
a promise, a tribute, a curse,
and they do not move.
I watch them from my window and wonder
what is the use of doing
if all I do is wait until the sun rises again?
Life is filled with bustling and buzzing but none
of it can matter
unless one day we stop
and we breathe
and we let our wings spread
and we sing our gratitudes.

# a haiku (2)

the clouds are heavy
i think i can hold them but
the rain keeps falling

# His Charming Ensign

I'm going to write a poem
so that I can show him
how I really, really know him
and prove how great I can be!
I suppose he won't expect it
and possibly reject it,
but I predict that he'll respect it
and fall forever in love with me.

but then I'll have to lose him,
befuddle him, confuse him,
at the very least bemuse him
and move on without a ring...
because if I'm being truthful
(and not a tad bit rueful)
my light fingers come in useful,
so he won't suspect a thing.

# Momento Mori

I thought I was invincible
Until the quiet of dawn cooled the mug in my
hand
And spelled my mortality out in the dew.

# Dandelion Seeds

Sometimes I grow in rich, rich soil and bloom
into a yellow sun-
others, I battle to survive in cracks against the
barraging wind, left to brave the raindrops that
bruise me so easily
often I am not alone
I have brothers, sisters, friends that sprout beside
me
but I cannot stay with them for long or else I will
find comfort
and settle where I land.
if I were made at all, I was made by sea-salt
winds.
Over and over, I die and am born again, and
each time I care too much.
Each version of me is buried beneath the same
sun as the last, and the same moonbeams stand
vigil over my graves.
What remains of me is carried,
uplifted by the storms that tore me down, and I
rise above them,
displaced but still wholeheartedly me,
merely a me aching to find myself again,
buried somewhere deep within the sea-salt
winds.

Life exchanges comfort for the chance to face the tempest; to emerge weathered and alive; to touch the skies and face the stars and to live longing only to do so again.

# Home is where the heart is

The curtains are closed
and yellow lights are on
and smeared windows are cracking
and red bricks are crumbling
and angry weeds are rising
and black vines are creeping
and they are clinging to the walls like a temper
and a grudge
and a promise.

The curtains are closed
and smoke curls from the chimney
and it is black and shapeless and solid
and it burns the eyes
and the noses
and the throats of cats prowling by,
and their whiskers twitch
(and they know they should leave
and they stay anyway).

The curtains are closed
and the smoke carries a fragmented song
and it smells of yesterday, almost twelve years
ago
and the windows are cracked

and the lights are on
and the song is played on heartstrings

and it is so very, very beautiful
and so very, very sad
and the curtains are closed, again.

# there was once a window

there was once a window
from which you could see the world
see every river, every stream,
every fox or bird.
And upon the redwood windowsill
your binoculars sat,
the strap of worn-down leather,
the lenses thick and fat.
I'd peer through the glass
and out into the world
beyond the eldest trees
to the freedom of the bird.
I'd watch the grass a-waving
to the ants so far below,
carrying everything they could,
doing more than they could know,
and then I'd move my gaze across
til it landed on your chair.
But now I can't seem to look away.
This time you're not there.

# The Mantra of the Fool

I believe that goodbyes are as temporary as they are final, and that they are what happens when life catches up with its missed deadlines.

I believe that goodbye is a lie, a cheat, and the most honest a person can be; that trusted goodbyes are said by shopkeepers, and saints, and teachers, and politicians, and only a fool would trust a single one of them.

I believe that goodbyes are what happens when you leave with the intention to return, and if you have no intention to return?

I believe you'll find one along the way in the shape of a heart, or a china doll called Mary, or the moon on a Tuesday evening in Liverpool.

I believe goodbyes are for the lovers and the haters and the fighters, and that goodbyes don't discredit little girls with plastic swords or little boys with flower crowns of daisies and dandelions.

I believe a goodbye is only finished on a deathbed, and that on a deathbed no goodbye is final because death is not the end, but the beginning of something new and unexplored to which we are yet to say hello.

But most of all, I believe goodbyes are what I deserve, and goodbyes are what I don't want- not one bit.'

So, until my final goodbye is thwarted again,
I will say hello to everybody I can,
and love as much as I dare,
and dare as much as I ought to be loved.

Milton Keynes UK
Ingram Content Group UK Ltd.
UKHW020939220424
441551UK00019B/1449